How to Get AAA Credit in 60 Days

JOSETTE HILL-WILSON

Quantity sales and special discounts are available on quantity purchases by corporations, associations, and others. For details, contact the publisher at the address above.

Orders by U.S. trade bookstores and wholesalers. Email info@ BeyondPublishing.net

The Beyond Publishing Speakers Bureau can bring authors to your live event. For more information or to book an event contact the Beyond Publishing Speakers Bureau speak@BeyondPublishing.net

The Author can be reached directly at BeyondPublishing.net

Manufactured and printed in the United States of America distributed globally by BeyondPublishing.net

New York | Los Angeles | London | Sydney

ISBN Hardcover: 978-1-63792-578-2
ISBN Softcover: 978-1-63792-579-9

TABLE OF CONTENTS

INTRODUCTION

Unfortunately, today, we live in a society that determines our net worth and value as a human being by the type of credit file we have. If your credit report is good, chances are you will receive and partake of some of the better things in life. But the opposite couldn't be more true if your credit report is bad. There are very few creditors who will extend credit to people with a bad credit profile.

But what if it wasn't your fault? What if you had to make the simple choice between eating and making your car payment? What if a job lay-off, a medical emergency, or some other personal crisis prevented you from making a timely payment? Should you be forced to pay for this for the next seven to ten years?

The credit bureaus are judge and jury in relation to your credit file. But there is one difference. A judge will at least give you the chance to defend yourself in court before passing judgment. And in America we are *supposed* to have a chance to face our accusers *before* judgment is passed. This is entirely untrue when it comes to your credit file.

The truth is that your creditors and the credit bureaus have been swapping information about you behind your back for a long time.

You are not asked or given any benefit of defense when this happens. It is, in fact, legal gossip!

The system, as it stands today, does not give you the opportunity to defend yourself before inscribing your credit file with negative information, even if it is not yours! You must prove to them that the negative information on your credit file is incorrect, invalid, or otherwise erroneous before they will remove it. That means in their eyes, you are *guilty* until proven *innocent*.

You might wonder how a system like this is allowed to operate in our *democracy*, in a country where we've been brought up to believe that a person is innocent until proven guilty. Why aren't we extended some courtesy by the credit bureaus? Why don't they give us a chance to defend ourselves before placing negative information on our credit files?

Good questions, aren't they? You may not like the answer though... *they don't have to!* The credit bureaus are private companies and corporations. They are in business to make a profit. And that profit comes from one place and one place only: *your creditors.*

Your creditors pay to see your credit file information and believe it to be true and correct. They also reciprocate by exchanging your credit information with the credit bureaus. So... your creditors pay the credit bureaus and the credit bureaus are in business to make a profit. Where do you fit in? You don't.

Unfortunately, you are just another number in the vast data bank of numbers. Your credit report and the information it contains are not important or of any consequence to anyone but you. That's why you are the only one who can do anything about it.

Well, my friend, that's why I put this information together and developed this unique program. I have seen too many people destroyed by the credit reporting system. I have watched helplessly by the wayside as their credit files were corrupted and their self-dignity was destroyed in the process.

So many people with poor credit have done their best to make timely payments but couldn't because of a personal problem or another. Should they pay for this both financially and emotionally for the next seven to ten years? I don't believe so. I believe everyone deserves a second chance. I believe that you deserve a second chance, no matter what the previous circumstances were. Put those problems behind you now. It's time to move on and re-establish a good credit file.

You can remove past negative information; it will take time and tenacity. The process is simple, but it's not easy. It will take some work on your part, but if you're serious about getting a second chance, you won't mind.

Improving your credit score can take time, but there are steps you can take to help boost your score in a relatively short period of time. Here are a few tips to help you get an A1 credit rating in 60 days:

1. **Pay all of your bills on time**. Late payments can have a major negative impact on your credit score. Make sure you pay all of your bills on time, and set reminders, if necessary.

2. **Keep your credit card balances low**. High credit card balances can negatively impact your credit score. Try to keep your credit card balances below 30 percent of your credit limit.

3. **Dispute any errors on your credit report.** Review your credit report and dispute any errors you find with the credit bureau.

4. **Increase your credit limit.** Ask your credit card issuer to increase your credit limit. This can help lower your credit utilization and improve your score.

5. **Use a secured credit card.** If you have no credit or bad credit, consider using a secured credit card to help establish a positive credit history.

6. **Consolidate your credit card debt.** Consider consolidating your credit card debt to lower your credit utilization and simplify your payments.

7. **Be patient.** Improving your credit score takes time and consistent efforts. Be patient and consistent in your efforts.

Congratulations! You are about to take the final steps necessary to begin a brand new life with good credit! Study the material, use the information, and get a new start!

HISTORY OF CONSUMER CREDIT

CHAPTER 1

Before you establish your new credit identity, it is important to understand how the credit reporting system works, how it operates, and how it affects you.

The roots of consumer credit go as far back as man can remember. It starts with someone or some business having a product or service to sell. Either the price of the product is beyond the reach of the average person or payment for the product is not convenient at the time of sale and that's what gives birth to a consumer credit program.

Take, for example, a moderately priced automobile at $13,500. The manufacturer, in order to make a profit, needs to sell many vehicles at this price. But how many of us can plop down $13,500 in one lump sum?

If the manufacturer only sold automobiles to people who could afford to pay in one lump sum, he would sell very few cars. Consequently, the price would skyrocket from $13,500 to let's say $113,500, due to the manufacturer's need to make an equitable profit. On the other hand, the manufacturer couldn't make any money if he sold the same automobile for $400.

So the manufacturer needs to sell the automobile at a price consistent with perceived value and quality, but still make it available to people who don't have the entire $13,500. That's why the automobile loan business is so big.

Let's take a look at another example. Actually, this next example is rooted deep in our history. When the payment for products or services is inconvenient at the time of sale, a merchant (or creditor) typically offers payment terms, usually within 30 days.

This type of consumer credit can be traced back to the general store days when a patron would typically pick up a few things, charge them to an open account, and agree to pay the entire account by the end of the month.

Those days are pretty much long gone, replaced by major credit cards and department store cards. But the principle is still the same. The only difference today is that theoretically, you never have to completely pay off a charge account. As long as you pay the interest on the account or the minimum payment, you can continue to charge to this account, up to the credit limit, without ever paying off the original debt. This is how a lot of people get into serious trouble and consequently damage their credit files almost irreparably.

As an evolution of this process, it was natural that some kind of credit reporting system would emerge.Creditors became concerned that they were doing business with a consumer who would repay their account in a timely fashion, and has proven timely repayment with other creditors as well.So, the credit bureaus were born and began to track credit information on individuals and businesses, selling that information to subscribers (creditors) and receiving information as well.

You should understand that the relationship between the credit bureau and the subscriber can (with your permission only) receive information about your current credit status. But, in exchange, the subscriber must provide payment history and account information to the credit bureau. This, however, transpires without your permission.

In other words, only you can authorize access to your credit file, but once you have, your creditor has carte blanche to report any credit information on your file he chooses, even if the information is incorrect!

The Credit Bureau System

Note that the credit bureaus are private, not government credit reporting companies. All three companies are listed on the New York Stock Exchange. They are in business to make money, just like any other business.

Their business is to store information reported by many creditors, and in turn, sell back credit bureau information to those same companies. The more credit data that the credit bureau can provide on any individual is to their advantage.

How Credit Bureaus Get Their Information

SUBSCRIBERS

Companies that subscribe to the credit bureaus' services send credit history to the credit bureau. Updates are periodically sent by the creditor to the credit bureau. It should be noted that since the creditors report at different times to each credit bureau, different amounts and dates can appear on each credit report. Many times this information is incorrectly and inaccurately reported.

Creditors that report to the credit bureau are most often banks, savings and loans, mortgage companies, large department stores, finance companies, Visa and MasterCard, banks, oil companies, and companies that are members of the credit bureau.

PUBLIC RECORDS

Credit bureaus also get their information from public records, such as the local courthouse. This information may include judgments, bankruptcies, tax liens, wage attachments, and notice of default on properties. It may be noted that the credit bureau may pick up from the public record a notice of default but later fail to record the correct information if the default was corrected.

MISSING INFORMATION

In reviewing your credit report, you may notice that much information is missing or inaccurate. The reason for missing information is that not all creditors belong to the credit bureau. For example, if you are paying off a bill with a small store, and they are not a member of the credit bureau, your good payments will not be reported on your credit report. For a small fee, you are able to list this good credit on your credit report.

WHAT IS A CREDIT CARD?

CHAPTER 2

A credit card is a great financial tool. It can be more convenient to use and carry than cash, and it offers valuable consumer protections under federal law.

At the same time, it's a big responsibility. If you don't use it carefully, you may owe more than you can repay, damage your credit rating, and create credit problems for yourself that can be difficult to undo.

Chances are your mail is full of solicitations from credit card issuers. How do you know if the time is right for a credit card? Here's some important information that may help you determine whether you're ready for plastic, what to look for when you select a company to do business with, and how to use your credit card responsibly.

Qualifying for a Credit Card

If you're at least 18 years old and have a regular source of income, you're well on your way to qualifying for a card. But despite the invitations from card issuers, you'll still have to demonstrate that you're a good risk before they grant you credit. The proof is in your credit record. If you've financed a car loan or other purchase, you probably have a record at a credit reporting bureau.

This credit history shows how responsible you've been in paying your bills and helps the credit card issuer decide how much credit to extend.

Before you submit a credit application, get a copy of your report to make sure it's accurate. It's available from the three major credit bureaus: Some websites may try to charge you money to see your credit score but to get a copy of your report is free.

- Equifax PO Box 105873, Atlanta, GA 30348; (800) 685-1111
- Experian (formerly TRW), PO Box 8030, Layton, UT 84041; (800) 392- 1122
- TransUnion PO Box 390, Springfield, PA 19064; (216) 779-7200

Establishing A Credit History

Suppose you haven't financed a car loan, a computer, or some other major purchase. How do you begin to establish credit? First, consider applying for a credit card at a local store and use it responsibly. Ask if they report to a credit bureau. If they do — and if you pay your bills on time— you'll establish a good credit history.

Second, consider a secured credit card. It requires that you open and maintain a bank account or other asset account at a financial institution as security for your line of credit. Your credit line will be a percentage of your deposit, typically from 50 to 100 percent. Application and processing fees are not uncommon for secured credit cards. In addition, secured credit cards usually carry higher interest rates than traditional non-secured cards.

Third, consider asking someone with an established credit history— perhaps a relative— to co-sign the account if you don't qualify for credit on your own. The co-signer promises to pay your debts if you don't. You'll want to repay any debt promptly, so you can build a credit history and apply for credit in the future on your own.

A positive credit history is an asset, not only when you apply for a credit card, but also when you apply for a job or insurance, or when you want to finance a car or home.

If Your Application is Denied

If you're turned down for a card, ask why. It may be that you haven't been at your current address or job long enough. Or that your income doesn't meet the issuer's criteria. Different credit card companies have different standards. But if you are turned down by several companies, it may indicate that you are not ready for a credit card.

If you've been denied credit because of information supplied by a credit bureau, federal law requires the creditor to give you the name and address of the bureau that supplied the information. If you contact that bureau within 30 days of receiving the denial, you are entitled to a free copy of your report. If your file contains accurate negative information, only time and good credit habits will restore your credit-worthiness. If you find an error in your report, you are entitled to have it investigated by the credit bureau and corrected at no charge.

Getting the Best Deal

Fees, charges, and benefits vary among credit card issuers. When you're choosing a credit card, shop around. Compare these important features:

Annual Percentage Rate (APR). The APR is a measure of the cost of credit, expressed as a yearly interest rate. Check out the "periodic rate," too. That's the rate the issuer applies to your outstanding balance to figure the finance charge for each billing period. For example, if you have an outstanding balance of $2,000, with 18.5 percent interest and a minimum monthly payment, it would take over 11 years to pay off the debt and cost you an additional $1,934 just for interest, which almost doubles the total cost of your original purchase.

Grace period. This is the time between the date of a purchase and the date interest starts being charged on that purchase. If your card has a standard grace period, you have an opportunity to avoid finance charges by paying your current balance in full. Some issuers allow a grace period for new purchases even if you do not pay your balance in full every month. If there is no grace period, the issuer imposes a finance charge from the date you use your card or from the date each transaction is posted to your account.

Annual fees. Many credit card issuers charge an annual fee for granting you credit, typically $15 to $55. Some issuers charge no annual fee.

Transaction fees and other charges. Some issuers charge a fee if you use the card to get a cash advance, if you fail to make a payment on time, or if you exceed your credit limit. Some may charge a flat fee every month whether you use the card or not.

Customer service. Many issuers have 24-hour toll-free telephone numbers.

Other benefits. Issuers may offer additional benefits, some with a cost, such as: insurance, credit card protection, discounts, rebates, and special merchandise offers.

Credi-quette

Once you get a card, sign it immediately, so no one else can use it. Note that the accompanying papers have important information, like customer service telephone numbers, in case your card is lost or stolen. File this information in a safe place.

Call the card issuer to activate the card. Many issuers require this step to minimize fraud and to give you additional information.

Keep your account information to yourself. Never give out your credit card number or expiration date over the phone unless you know who you're dealing with. A criminal can use this information to steal money from you, or even assume your credit identity.

Keep copies of sales slips and compare charges when your bill arrives. Promptly report in writing any questionable charges to the card issuer.

Don't lend your card to anyone, even to a friend. Your credit privilege and history are too precious to risk.

You're Responsible

While a credit card makes it easy to buy something now and pay for it later, you can lose track of how much you've spent by the time the bill arrives if you're not careful. And if you don't pay your bill in full, you'll probably have to pay finance charges on the unpaid balance.

What's more, if you continue to charge while carrying an outstanding balance, your debt can snowball. Before you know it, your minimum payment is only covering the interest. If you start having trouble repaying the debt, you could tarnish your credit report. And that can have a sizable impact on your life. A negative report can make it more difficult to finance a car or home, get insurance, and even get a job.

Federal protections. Federal law offers the following protections when you use credit cards.

Errors on Your Bill.

You must notify the card issuer in writing within 60 days after the first bill containing the error was mailed to you. In you letter, include your name; account number; the type, date, and amount of the error; and the reason why you believe the bill contains an error. In return, the card issuer must investigate the problem and either correct the error or explain to you why the bill is correct. This must occur within two billing cycles and not later than 90 days after the issuer receives your billing error notice. You do not have to pay the amount in question during the investigation.

Unauthorized Charges.

If your credit card is used without your authorization, you can be held liable for up to $50 per card. If you report the loss of a card before it is used, the card issuer cannot hold you responsible for any unauthorized charges. If a thief uses your card before you report it missing, the most you will owe for unauthorized charges is $50. You should be prompt in reporting the loss or theft of your card to limit your liability.

Kinds of Credit Accounts

Credit grantors generally use three types of accounts:

Revolving agreement. A consumer pays in full each month or chooses to make a partial payment based on the outstanding balance. Department stores, gas and oil companies, and banks typically issue credit cards based on a revolving credit plan.

Charge agreement. A consumer promises to pay the full balance each month, so the borrower does not have to pay interest charges. Charge cards, not credit cards, and charge accounts with local businesses often require repayment on this basis.

Installment agreement. A consumer signs a contract to repay a fixed amount of credit in equal payments over a specific period of time. Automobiles, furniture, and major appliances often are financed this way. Personal loans usually are paid back in installments, too.

HOW CREDIT SCORING WORKS

CHAPTER 3

The first thing you need to know about your credit score is that you don't have a credit score: you have many, and they change all the time.

Credit scores are designed to be a snapshot of your credit picture—typically, the picture that's contained in your credit report. New information is constantly being added to your report, and old information is being deleted. Those changes affect your score.

Credit scoring is a system used by lenders and financial institutions to evaluate an individual's creditworthiness. A credit score is a numerical representation of an individual's credit history, and it is based on the information in their credit report.

The most widely used credit score model is the FICO score, which ranges from 300 to 850. The higher the score, the better the creditworthiness. The FICO score is calculated based on five factors: payment history, credit utilization, length of credit history, new credit, and credit mix.

1. **Payment history**: This factor looks at whether you have made your payments on time and whether you have any outstanding

debts in collection. Late payments, missed payments, and bankruptcies can negatively impact your score.

2. **Credit utilization:** This factor looks at how much of your available credit you are using. A high credit utilization ratio can negatively impact your score.

3. **Length of credit history:** This factor looks at how long you have had credit and how long your credit accounts have been open. A longer credit history can be beneficial for your score.

4. **New credit:** This factor looks at how many new credit accounts you have opened recently and how many credit inquiries you have. Applying for too much credit in a short period of time can negatively impact your score.

5. **Credit mix:** This factor looks at the types of credit accounts you have, such as credit cards, mortgages, and personal loans. Having a mix of credit types can be beneficial for your score.

Lenders and financial institutions use credit scores as a tool to evaluate an individual's creditworthiness and decide whether to approve a loan or credit application. It's important to note that credit scoring is a complex process and the specific algorithms used to calculate credit scores are kept confidential to prevent manipulation.

More on Credit Scoring

Credit scoring is a system used to evaluate an individual's creditworthiness, and it plays a significant role in determining whether a person can qualify for a loan or credit card. There are several different credit scoring models, the most widely used is the FICO score, which ranges from 300 to 850.

FICO scores are based on the information in an individual's credit report, which is a record of their credit history. Credit reports are maintained by the three major credit reporting agencies: Experian, Equifax, and TransUnion. They gather information from various sources, such as banks, credit card companies, and other financial institutions, to create a comprehensive credit report.

The FICO score is calculated based on five factors: payment history, credit utilization, length of credit history, new credit, and credit mix.

1. **Payment history**: This factor looks at whether you have made your payments on time and whether you have any outstanding debts in collection. Late payments, missed payments, and bankruptcies can negatively impact your score.

2. **Credit utilization:** This factor looks at how much of your available credit you are using. A high credit utilization ratio can negatively impact your score.

3. **Length of credit history:** This factor looks at how long you have had credit and how long your credit accounts have been open. A longer credit history can be beneficial for your score.

4. **New credit**: This factor looks at how many new credit accounts you have opened recently and how many credit inquiries you have. Applying for too much credit in a short period of time can negatively impact your score.

5. **Credit mix**: This factor looks at the types of credit accounts you

have, such as credit cards, mortgages, and personal loans. Having a mix of credit types can be beneficial for your score.

It's important to note that credit scoring models are not static. They are regularly updated and improved to ensure they accurately reflect an individual's creditworthiness. Additionally, different lenders and financial institutions may use different credit scoring models or have different credit score requirements. Therefore, it's important to understand your credit score and credit history, and to work to improve it if necessary, to increase your chances of being approved for loans and credit.

That can be good news or bad news. The good news is that if you have a bad score now, you're not stuck with it forever. You can do a lot to improve your situation and make yourself more creditworthy in lenders' eyes.

The bad news is that you can't rest on your laurels. When you have a good score, you need to constantly monitor your credit to make sure it stays that way.

You also should know that there's more than one credit-scoring system out there. In fact, currently more than 100 credit-scoring models are being marketed to lenders. The best-known credit-scoring model, the FICO, is designed to predict whether a borrower will default. But credit-scoring systems have been created to do all of the following:

- Detect fraud in credit or insurance applications
- Calculate the amount of profit a credit card issuer is likely to make on a particular account
- Predict the risk of a specific kind of default, such as bankruptcy

- Forecast the probability that a policyholder will cost an insurer money

- Anticipate the risk that a consumer will default on a certain type of account, such as an auto loan, a mortgage, a cellular phone account, or a utility bill

- Estimate how much a borrower is likely to pay, if anything, on a delinquent account

- Anticipate which customers might close a credit card account or pay the balance down to zero

- Predict the likelihood that someone will respond to a direct-mail credit card solicitation

The vast majority of these scoring systems are developed by the same company that created the FICO: Fair Isaac Corporation. In addition, the credit bureaus and some outside companies have created their own formulas.

All that being said, you're much more likely to be affected by a FICO score than any other type of credit score. FICO is the industry leader. It's used in literally billions of lending decisions each year, including 75 percent of mortgage-lending assessments.

That's why the information in this chapter and elsewhere is based on how the FICO formula calculates your score. Other formula designs might differ somewhat in their details, but the behaviors that help and hurt your score are pretty consistent across the various systems.

Here are some other facts about credit scoring that you should keep in mind:

- You need to have and use credit to have a credit score—The classic FICO formulas need at least one account on your credit report that has been open for six months and one account that's been updated in the past six months. (It can be the same account.) If your credit history is too thin, or you've stopped using credit for a period of time, there might not be enough current data in your file to create a regular credit score. (That doesn't mean you can't be "scored." In mid-2004, Fair Isaac introduced the FICO Expansion Score for lenders who want to evaluate people with thin or nonexistent credit histories. This new score uses nontraditional information sources such as companies that monitor bounced checks.)

- A credit score usually isn't the only thing lenders consider—In mortgage-lending decisions, in particular, lenders may weigh a lot of other information, including your employment history and stability, the value of the property you're buying or refinancing, your income, and your total monthly debt payments as a percentage of that income, among other factors.

- So, although credit scores can be a powerful force in lending decisions, they might not be the sole determinant of whether you get credit.

- Credit-scoring systems were designed for lenders, not consumers—In other words, scores weren't created to be easy to understand. The actual formulas, and many of the details of how they work, are closely guarded trade secrets.

The credit-scoring companies don't want the process to be transparent or predictable, as discussed in the preceding chapter. They fear that letting out too many details would allow competitors to copy their formulas. They also worry that their formulas would lose their ability to predict risk if consumers knew exactly how to beat them.

We know more about the formulas than ever before, and certainly enough for you to improve your score. But given the number of variables involved and the mystery still surrounding credit scoring, you may not be able to forecast exactly how every action will affect a score, or how quickly.

WHAT IS A GOOD SCORE?

CHAPTER 4

One of the first questions many people have about credit scoring is what score lenders consider "good." There is, however, no single answer to that question.

Generally, of course, the higher the score, the better. Each lender makes its own decision about where to draw the line, based on how much risk it wants to take and how much profit it thinks it can make with a given blend of customers. Many lenders don't have a single cutoff but may have many, with each segment qualifying for different rates and terms. Finally, as noted earlier, a credit score is usually only one factor in the lending decision. Although scores typically have a big influence, a lender might decide that other factors are more important.

You can see from this national distribution chart of FICO credit scores that most of the U.S. population has a FICO score of 700 or higher. Many lenders use 700 or 720 as the cutoff for giving borrowers their best rates and terms. Many also use 620 as a cutoff point. Companies that deal with borrowers below that level are often called "subprime" lenders because their riskier borrowers are considered less than "prime."

FICO Credit Score Percent with Score

300–499 2%

500–549 5%

550–599 8%

600–649 12%

650–699 15%

700–749 18%

750–799 27%

800–850 13%

Your Credit Report: The Building Blocks for Your Score

Because your score is constructed from the information in your credit report, it's worth looking at what you'll find there.

In addition to identifying information about you—your name, address, and Social Security number—your report lists the following:

- Your credit accounts—Sometimes called "trade lines," these include loans, credit cards, and other credit accounts you've opened. Your report lists the type of account, how long ago you opened it, your balances, and details of your payment history.

- Requests for your credit—These are known as "inquiries," and there are basically two kinds. When you apply for credit, you authorize the lender to view your credit history. This is known as a "hard inquiry" and can affect your credit score. You might also see inquiries that you didn't initiate. These "soft inquiries" are typically made when a lender orders your credit report to make you a preapproved credit offer. Such marketing efforts don't affect your score.

- Public records and collections—These can include collection accounts, bankruptcies, tax liens, foreclosures, wage garnishments, lawsuits, and judgments.

Public records are culled from state and county courthouses. Lenders or collection agencies report most of the other information in your report.This data is collected, stored, and updated by credit bureaus, which are private, for-profit companies. The three major credit bureaus are Equifax, Experian (formerly known as TRW), and TransUnion, and their business is selling information about you to lenders.

Because they're competitors, the bureaus typically don't share information, and not all lenders report information to all three bureaus. In fact, if you get copies of your credit reports from the bureaus on the same day, you're likely to notice at least a few differences among them. An account that's listed on one credit bureau's report might not show up on the others, for example, or the balances showing on your various accounts might differ from bureau to bureau.

Because your score is based on the information that's in your report at a given credit bureau, the number differs depending on which bureau's credit report is used.Also, each time you or a lender "pulls" your score (in other words, orders a score to be calculated), it's likely to be at least somewhat different, because the information on which it's based has probably changed. Fair Isaac says most people's scores don't change all that much in a short period, but about 25 percent of consumers can expect to see their scores at a single bureau vary by more than 20 points over a three-month stretch.

There are time limits to what can appear on your credit report. Although positive information can appear indefinitely, negative marks—late payments, collection actions, and foreclosures—by federal law generally must be removed after seven years. Bankruptcies can be reported for ten years. Inquiries should be deleted in two years.

How Your Score Is Calculated

When most of us think of scores, we think of the relatively straightforward systems used in sports or in school tests. You get points (and possibly demerits) for certain actions, behaviors, or answers, and those are totaled to determine your score.

Credit scoring isn't nearly so easy. Credit-scoring models use "multi-variate" formulas. That basically means that the value of any given bit of information in your report might depend on other bits of information.

To understand how this works, let's use a noncredit example. Suppose that your sister calls you to report that her husband is more than an hour late in coming home from work, and she asks whether you think he's having an affair. To answer the question, you would need to review what you know about this man, including his attitude about his family, his general moral standards, and whether he's had dalliances in the past. Using all these variables, you could try to predict whether your brother-in-law is likely to be stepping out—or might just have stopped off to buy his wife an anniversary present.

Let's suppose that your brother-in-law is a stand-up guy. But you've personally observed your neighbor in a clinch with a woman who was not his wife. If your neighbor was an hour late in coming home and his wife asked you your opinion of his likely faithfulness, you might reach quite a different conclusion. So the same behavior—

coming home late—could evoke two very different predictions based on the information at your disposal.

The number of factors that the FICO formulas evaluate is infinitely greater, so you can see how difficult it can be sometimes to predict the outcomes of certain behaviors.

There's one thing that's always true, though: The FICO model is set up to place more value on current behavior than on past behavior. That means that the effect of your old credit troubles lessens over time if you start handling credit more responsibly.

However, the scores are also designed to react strongly to any signs that an once-good risk might be turning bad. That's why someone with a good score might suffer more heavily from a late payment.

It's generally a lot easier to lose points on your score than it is to gain them back, which is why it's so important to know how to improve and protect your score.

The Five Most Important Factors

Now that you understand in general how credit scores are calculated, we can move on to some specifics. The following are the five main factors that affect your FICO score according to their relative level of importance, along with a percentage figure that reflects how heavily that factor is weighed in calculating FICO scores for the general population. Each factor might weigh more or less heavily in your individual score, depending on your credit situation.

Your Payment History

This makes up about 35 percent of the typical score. It makes sense: your record of paying bills says a lot about how responsible you are with credit. Lenders want to know whether you pay on time and how long it's been since you've been late, if ever.

To put this in perspective: more than half of Americans don't have a single late payment on their credit reports, according to Fair Isaac, and only three in ten have ever been 60 days or more overdue in the past seven years.

When it comes to negative marks like late payments, the score focuses on three factors:

- **Recency**—This is how recently the borrower got into trouble. The more time that's passed since the credit problem, the less it affects a score.

- **Frequency**—As you might expect, someone who has had just one or two late payments typically looks better to lenders than someone who has had a dozen.

- **Severity**—There's a definite "hierarchy of badness" when it comes to your credit score. A payment that's 30 days late isn't considered as serious as one that's 60 or 120 days late. Collections, tax liens, and bankruptcy are among the biggest black marks.

If you've never been late, your clean history will help your score. But that doesn't mean you'll get a "perfect" score. A good credit history involves a lot more.

How Much You Owe

This equates to 30 percent of your score. The score looks at the total amount owed on all accounts, as well as how much you owe on different types of accounts (credit card, auto loan, mortgages, and so on).

To put this in perspective: most Americans use less than 30 percent of their available credit limits, according to Fair Isaac. Only one in secen uses 80 percent or more of available limits.

As you might expect, using a much higher percentage of your limits will worry lenders and potentially hurt your score. People who max out their credit limits, or even come close, tend to have a much higher rate of default than people who keep their credit use under control.

When it comes to revolving debt—credit cards and lines of credit—the credit score formula looks at the difference between your credit limits on the accounts and your balance, or the amount of credit you're actually using. The bigger the gap between your balance and your limit, the better.

Here's a point that needs clarification: lenders report your balances to the credit bureaus on a given day (usually each month, but sometimes only every other month or quarterly). It doesn't matter whether you pay the balance off in full the next day—the balance you owed on the reporting day is what shows up on your credit report. That's why people who pay off their credit cards in full every month still might have balances showing on their reports.

So you need to be careful with how much you charge, even if you never carry a balance from month to month. Your total balance during the month should never approach your credit limit if you want a good score.

The score also looks at how much you owe on installment loans (mortgages, auto loans) compared to what you originally borrowed. Paying down the balances over time tends to help your score.

How Long You've Had Credit

This is 15 percent of your total score. As such, it's generally much less important than the previous two factors, but it still matters. You can have a good score with a short history, but typically the longer you've had credit, the better.

To put this in perspective: the average American's oldest account has been established for about 14 years, according to Fair Isaac. One in four has an account that's been established for 20 years or more.

The score considers both of the following:

- The age of your oldest account
- The average age of all your accounts

Your Last Application for Credit

This is 10 percent of your overall score. Opening new accounts can ding your credit score, particularly if you apply for lots of credit in a short time and you don't have a long credit history.

To put this in perspective: the average American has not opened an account in 20 months.

The score factors in the following:

- How many accounts you've applied for recently
- How many new accounts you've opened

- How much time has passed since you applied for credit

- How much time has passed since you opened an account

You might have heard that "shopping around" for credit can hurt your score. We deal with this issue more thoroughly in Chapter 4, "Improving Your Score—The Right Way," but the FICO formula takes into account that people tend to shop around for important loans such as mortgages and auto financing. As long as you do your shopping in a fairly concentrated period of time, it shouldn't affect the score used for your application.

Also, pulling your own credit report and score doesn't affect your score. So long as you do it yourself, ordering from a credit bureau or a reputable intermediary, the inquiry won't count against you. If you have a lender pull your score "just to see it," though, you could end up hurting your score.

The Types of Credit You Use

This is 10 percent of your score. The FICO scoring formula wants to see a "healthy mix" of credit, but Fair Isaac is customarily vague about what that means.

The company does say that you don't need to have a loan of each possible type—credit card, mortgage, auto loan, and so on—to have a good score. Furthermore, you're cautioned against applying for credit you don't need in an effort to boost your score, because that can backfire.

To get the highest possible scores, however, you need to have both revolving debts like credit cards and installment debts like an auto loan, mortgage, or personal loan. These latter loans don't have to still be open to influence your score. But they do still need to show up on your credit report.

Bankcards—major credit cards such as Visa, MasterCard, American Express, Discover, and Diner's Club—are typically better for your credit score than department store or other "finance company" cards. (Department stores' cards are typically issued by finance companies, which specialize in consumer lending and which, unlike banks, don't receive deposits.)

Installment loans can reflect well on you, too. That's because lenders generally require more documentation and take a closer look at your credit before granting the loan.

To put this in perspective: the average American has thirteen credit accounts showing on their credit report, including nine credit cards and four installment loans, according to Fair Isaac.

Your Credit Scorecard

How these five factors are weighed when it comes to you—as opposed to the general population—depends on a little-known sorting system known at Fair Isaac as "scorecards."

Scorecards allow the FICO formula to segment borrowers into one of ten different groups, based on information in their credit reports.

If the credit history shows only positive information, the model takes into account the following:

- The number of accounts
- The age of the accounts
- The age of the youngest account

If the history shows a serious delinquency, the model looks for these:

- The presence of any public record, such as a bankruptcy or tax lien

- The worst delinquency, if there's more than one on the file

After the model has this information, it decides which of the ten score-cards to assign. Although Fair Isaac keeps the details pretty secret, it's known that there is at least one scorecard for people with a bankruptcy in their backgrounds, and another for people who don't have much information in their reports.

Grouping people this way is supposed to enhance the formula's predictive power. The theory is that the same behavior in different borrowers can mean different things. Someone with a troubled credit history who suddenly opens a slew of accounts, for example, might be seen as a much greater risk that someone with a long, clean history. Scorecards allow the FICO formula to give different weight to the same information.

Sometimes, however, the actual results of the scorecards can be a little bizarre.

YOUR CREDIT SCORE

Although all three bureaus use the FICO scoring model, the actual formula differs slightly from bureau to bureau. That's because the way the bureaus collect and report data isn't exactly the same. It's unlikely that these differences would have much impact on your score, but you should know that they exist. You're much more likely, though, to have different scores from bureau to bureau because the underlying information is different.

As discussed earlier, lenders can have their own in-house scoring formulas in addition to, or instead of, using FICO scores. Lenders also can use different "editions" of the FICO formula. Just as not everyone updates to the latest computer operating systems when they're released, not every lender uses the latest versions of credit-scoring formulas.

Older versions of the FICO formula, for example, counted participation in a credit-counseling program as a negative factor; newer versions view it as a neutral factor. So, if you're currently in a debt management program, you might be viewed more negatively by some lenders than by others.

You can help protect yourself somewhat from these discrepancies by being preapproved for a home loan before you start house shopping. But this is just another reason why it's important to improve and protect your score. The higher your score is, the less you have to worry about a few points making a difference.

THE IMPORTANCE OF PAYMENT HISTORY

CHAPTER 5

Your payment history is the most key factor that determines your credit score. Past due payments, collections, and bankruptcies will have a negative impact on your score. On the other hand, making payments on time will boost your score. To build good credit, it is essential to make all your payments on time. Your payment history is one of the most key factors that determine your credit score. It accounts for 35 percent of your FICO score and is used to determine your creditworthiness. Your payment history reflects how well you have paid your debts in the past and is used to predict how well you will pay your debts in the future.

Lenders look at your payment history to see if you have a history of making payments on time or if you have a history of late or missed payments. Past due payments can have a negative impact on your credit score and can result in additional fees and charges.

It is important to make all your payments on time, as a late payment can stay on your credit report for up to seven years. Even one overdue payment can have a negative impact on your credit score, so it's important to make sure that you pay all your bills on time, every time.

In addition to paying all your bills on time, it's also important to avoid maxing out your credit cards. Keeping your credit utilization low is another crucial factor in maintaining a good credit score.

To maintain a good payment history, you can set up automatic payments for your bills, make sure you have enough funds in your account to cover your bills, and always pay at least the minimum amount due on your credit card bills. It is also a clever idea to keep track of your bills and due dates using a budgeting app or calendar.

Payment history is a crucial factor in determining your credit score and creditworthiness. It is important to make all your payments on time, avoid maxing out your credit cards, and track your bills to ensure that you always pay on time. By maintaining a good payment history, you can improve your credit score and increase your chances of getting approved for loans and credit cards with favorable terms.

The Role of Credit Utilization

Your credit utilization, or the amount of credit you are using compared to the amount of credit available to you, also plays a role in determining your credit score. Lenders want to see that you are not maxing out your credit cards and that you are using credit responsibly. To improve your credit utilization, try to keep your balances low and pay them off in full each month. Credit utilization, also known as the debt-to-credit ratio, is the amount of credit you are using compared to the amount of credit available to you. It is calculated by taking the total amount of credit you are using and dividing it by the total amount of credit available to you. This ratio is used to determine how much of your available credit you are using and is a major factor in determining your credit score.

A high credit utilization ratio indicates that you are using a lot of your available credit and may be a sign of financial stress. This can have a negative impact on your credit score, as it suggests that you may be overextending yourself financially. On the other hand, a low credit utilization ratio indicates that you are using a small amount of your available credit, which is considered a positive sign of financial stability.

It is recommended to keep your credit utilization ratio below 30 percent. This means that you should use no more than 30 percent of your available credit at any given time. For example, if you have a credit limit of $10,000, you should aim to keep your balance at or below $3,000.

To improve your credit utilization ratio, you can take several steps such as:

- Pay off high-interest credit card debt as soon as possible
- Keep your credit card balances low
- Request a credit limit increase from your credit card issuer
- Space out your credit card applications
- Consider consolidating your credit card debt

It is important to keep in mind that your credit utilization ratio is just one of many factors that goes into determining your credit score. While it is important to keep your credit utilization ratio low, it is also important to focus on other factors such as payment history and the length of your credit history.

Credit utilization is a key factor in determining your credit score. It is important to keep your credit utilization ratio low by paying off high-interest credit card debt, keeping your credit card balances low, requesting a credit limit increase, spacing out your credit card applications, and consolidating your credit card debt. By managing your credit utilization ratio effectively, you can improve your credit score and increase your chances of getting approved for loans and credit cards with favorable terms.

Here is how you get AAA credit in 60 days or less……

Good credit is everyone's dream. A wise use of credit can go a long way. It certainly makes certain goals in life (like acquiring a business loan from a bank) easily attainable. But the key question remains: "What does it take to achieve 'Triple A' credit?"

First and foremost, let me set the record straight. The Bible clearly states that when money is borrowed, it needs to be repaid. Psalms 37:21. "The *wicked* borrows and does not pay back, but the righteous is generous and gives." It is not good to borrow and not repay; this is what causes you to have bad credit in the first place. Whatever you do in one area of your life is a reflection of the other areas of your life. It is important, and it is critical to point out where most people go wrong when it comes to their credit and credit report.

People with bad credit will usually seek credit repair help. Most would seek credit expert advice, and few will try to do it themselves by purchasing a credit repair book.

Mainly, the problem is not the type of help you hire, rather the assumption you are left with after the whole credit repair process. Where most people go wrong is that once their credit report is free of any negative entries (or errors), they simply assume that they now have an excellent credit. That's simply untrue.

In reality, your credit is not bad because you now have managed to erase the negative entries that was shown previously on your credit report. At the same time, you do not have 'Triple A' credit either, unless you have positive items or entries showing on your credit report. You must replace the negatives with positives to get Triple-A credit.

And the key to a successful credit repair is not just getting rid of the negative entries on your credit report, but, rather, to show off that you have multiple positive entries on your credit report that can buy the confidence of your bank to loan you their money.

You can find numerous articles dedicated to guiding you through the credit repair process, but few will discuss further than just repairing your credit. Meaning few will tell you (better yet, know about).

How to **add positive entries to your credit report**?

And Get Triple A Credit in 60 Days

It is very important you understand that you can repair your own credit and make it flawless, better than anyone ever could. Today, there is so much help on credit repair, but not all are legitimate help,and it is extremely important to keep that in mind.

If you want to avoid getting chopped down by bogus repair companies, take the following two statements as an advice that will serve you a long way.

1. There is no law available to any credit repair company, expert, or attorney that is not available to you as the credit consumer.

2. Credit repair companies use the same law made available to you by Congress to repair your bad credit. And they certainly can not change the law for their clients.

The above two simple statements might seem obvious, but repeating them like a mantra can be the difference between getting ripped off and getting the 'Triple A' credit you deserve.

Here you will learn two powerful and proven ways that will give you a sterling credit in the shortest time possible: 25 days. Apply the following two techniques and, guaranteed, you will give your credit a facelift that will cause banks to open their checkbook.

1. A millionaire's credit in 60 days.

Phase 1: Do you have a checking account and a savings account? Good. If you don't, no worries— these days, you can open an account online. It should take you no more than five minutes. You got your accounts opened? Good. Now comes the second phase.

Phase 2: Now you will need your savings account to use it as collateral. Now, using your savings account, ask your bank for a secured passbook loan (or signature loan).

You can borrow a dollar for dollar with a passbook loan. This type of loan works well with as little as $300, but if you have $10,000, that's even better. Once you secure a loan with a passbook, you can not touch the funds until you have fully repaid the loan. Remember, you should be able to do without these funds for 30 days. A bank secured with your passbook loan has no risk in lending you money, so any bank should be willing.

Note: It is extremely important that the bank reports your loans to the credit bureau. Therefore, ask your bank if they report your payment history to the three credit bureaus. It is critical part of this whole process. After all, the whole purpose of you doing this is to add zing to your credit report with a very powerful and positive payment history, right?

Now, once you borrow the money, wait 25 days and repay the loan back to your bank. Because you have fully repaid your loan, the bank will send your positive payment history to the credit bureau. You can do this with three to five banks at a time.

That's a grand slam!

Now, you have the bank as your friend and the credit bureaus cannot help it but report your good payment history.

2. How to turn $500 - $1,000 into a millionaire's credit.

With let's say a $1,000 in your account, ask the loan officer for a 12-month $1,000 passbook loan. Do not be discouraged; you can certainly achieve this with less money, but if you can afford to do it, don't hesitate.

By the time you're done with this techni2ue— well, it'll be all worth it. Just wait and see. Since this is a secured passbook loan (meaning, it is secured by the amount of money available in your savings), most banks will not run a credit check. And if they tried to do so, explain to them why they should not, as it is secured by the money you already have in your savings account, which you won't be able to access until you pay off your loan anyway, so there is no justified reason to run a credit check. Now with the $1,000 secured passbook loan from your first bank, open a savings account at another bank with the $1,000 loan received from the first bank.

Request that they give you a $1,000 12-month loan and do not mention the loan received from the first bank. Wait about a week or two, go to a third bank and repeat the process.

Next, at one of the three banks, open a checking account with the $1,000 you received from the third bank. You now have a$1,000 in a checking account and three outstanding 12-month loans at three different banks – for a total of $3,000. Deduct your original $1,000 and you need only repay $2,000 plus interest.

Note: make sure that you ask your bank if they have a pre-payment penalty because you do not want that.

Finally, about one week later, start to pre-pay your three loans.

Now you have an advance payment record with three banks and will have established powerful credit for your credit report. From now on, every type of loan and credit card will be yours for the asking.

Here you are with untouchable credit, three big banks as your future business friends, and a credit bureau reporting positive payment history – all in just under 60 days. You just learned about one of the very few techniques that can change your credit significantly within a month's time.

Of course, you can apply these techniques for as long as you like and keep improving your credit. Apply these techniques discussed, and you will get the Triple A credit you deserve.

Building Credit with Other Types of Loans

Another way to build credit is to take out a loan. Installment loans, such as auto loans or personal loans, can help you build credit. When you take out a loan, the lender will report your payments to the credit bureaus. As you make payments on time, your credit score will improve. In addition to using a credit card, another way to build credit is by taking out a loan. A loan is an amount of money that you borrow from a lender and agree to pay back over time, usually with interest. When you take out a loan and make your payments on time, it can help to improve your credit score.

There are many types of loans that can help you build credit, such as personal loans, student loans, and auto loans. Each type of loan has its own unique requirements, terms, and conditions, so it's important to research and understand the options available to you before applying for a loan.

Personal loans are unsecured loans that you can use for a variety of purposes, such as consolidating credit card debt, paying for home improvements, or making a large purchase. Personal loans usually have fixed interest rates and a set repayment term, usually between one and five years.

Student loans are loans that are designed to help students pay for their education. These loans can be either federal or private, and they usually have low interest rates and flexible repayment terms.

Auto loans are loans that are used to purchase a vehicle. These loans usually have a set repayment term, usually between three and six years, and a fixed interest rate.

When you apply for a loan, the lender will typically check your credit score and credit history to determine whether you are a good candidate for credit. If you have no credit history or a limited credit history, you may be considered a higher risk, and may be offered a secured loan or a credit-builder loan.

A secured loan is a type of loan where the borrower pledges an asset, such as a car or a house, as collateral for the loan. The asset serves as collateral for the loan, which means that the lender is less at risk of losing money if you default on your payments.

A credit-builder loan is a type of loan that is designed to help people establish credit history. The lender holds the loan funds in an account and releases them to you after you make a certain number of payments. This type of loan can help to establish credit history and improve your credit score.

It's important to keep in mind that taking out a loan, like a credit card, can also have a negative impact on your credit score if you don't make your payments on time or if you take on too much debt. It's important to only borrow what you can afford to pay back and to make sure you understand the terms and conditions of the loan before you apply.

In conclusion, taking out a loan can be a great way to build credit. By borrowing money and making your payments on time, you can establish a positive credit history that will help you qualify for loans and other credit products in the future. As with credit cards, it's important to borrow responsibly, and only borrow what you can afford to pay back, to avoid negative impacts on your credit score. Building credit takes time and effort, but by being responsible and taking steps to improve your credit score, you can achieve a good credit history that will open up many financial opportunities for you in the future.

Other Factors that Affect Your Credit Score

There are other factors that can affect your credit score, such as the length of your credit history and the types of credit you have. A longer credit history and a mix of different types of credit (such as a mortgage, a credit card, and an auto loan) can help improve your credit score. In addition to payment history and credit utilization, there are several other factors that can affect your credit score. These factors include:

1. **Credit age:** The length of your credit history can affect your credit score. A longer credit history can be seen as a positive factor because it shows that you have a track record of managing credit responsibly.

2. **Credit mix:** Having a mix of different types of credit, such as a mortgage, credit card, and auto loan, can be seen as a positive factor because it shows that you can handle different types of credit responsibly.

3. **Inquiries:** Every time you apply for credit, an inquiry is made on your credit report. These inquiries can have a negative impact on your credit score, especially if you have multiple inquiries in a short period of time.

4. **Credit utilization:** As mentioned earlier, credit utilization is the amount of credit you are using compared to the amount of credit available to you. A high credit utilization can have a negative impact on your credit score.

5. **Credit report errors:** Sometimes, credit reports can contain errors, such as incorrect information or duplicate accounts. It's

important to check your credit report regularly and dispute any errors you find.

6. **Public records:** Public records, such as bankruptcies, foreclosures, or tax liens, can have a negative impact on your credit score.

It's important to note that not all credit scoring models weigh these factors equally, and different credit scoring models can have different ranges for what is considered a "good" credit score. However, by understanding these factors and taking steps to improve them, you can improve your credit score over time.

It's also important to keep in mind that credit scores are not permanent and can change over time. By monitoring your credit score regularly and taking steps to improve it, you can achieve a good credit score and open up many financial opportunities for you in the future.

Understanding the factors that affect your credit score is an important step in managing your credit and building a good credit history. By taking steps to improve your payment history, credit utilization, credit mix, and disputing any errors on your credit report, you can improve your credit score and access more financial opportunities. Remember that credit score is not permanent, you can always work on it and improve it over time.

How to Fix Bad Credit

If you have bad credit, it can be challenging to secure loans or credit cards with favorable terms. However, it is possible to improve your credit score over time by taking the following steps:

1. **Check your credit report:** The first step in fixing bad credit is to check your credit report for errors. Dispute any errors you find with the credit bureau that issued the report.

2. **Make payments on time:** Late payments can have a major impact on your credit score. To improve your credit score, make sure to pay all of your bills on time.

3. **Reduce your credit card balances:** High credit card balances can negatively impact your credit score. Try to pay down your credit card balances as much as possible.

4. **Limit new credit applications:** Each time you apply for new credit, it results in a hard inquiry on your credit report, which can temporarily lower your credit score. Limit the number of new credit applications you make.

5. **Keep old credit accounts open:** The length of your credit history can affect your credit score, so it's best to keep old credit accounts open.

6. **Look into credit counseling:** Credit counseling can help you develop a plan to pay down debt and improve your credit score.

7. **Be patient:** Improving your credit score takes time, so it's important to be patient. It can take several months or even years to see a significant improvement in your credit score.

8. **Consider a secured credit card:** Secured credit cards are a great way to rebuild credit. These cards require a security deposit, but they report to the credit bureaus just like a regular credit card.

It's also important to keep in mind that credit scores are not permanent and can change over time. By monitoring your credit score regularly and taking steps to improve it, you can achieve a good credit score and open up many financial opportunities for you in the future.

Bad credit can be a major obstacle when it comes to securing loans or credit cards with favorable terms, but it's not a permanent condition. By understanding the factors that affect your credit score, and taking the steps to improve it, you can fix your bad credit and achieve a good credit score. Remember that rebuilding credit takes time, and you need to be patient and consistent in your efforts. There are several other things to keep in mind when trying to fix bad credit:

1. **Prioritize high-interest debt:** High-interest debt, such as credit card debt, can have a significant impact on your credit score. Prioritize paying off this type of debt to improve your credit score.

2. **Consider a debt consolidation loan:** If you have a lot of high-interest debt, a debt consolidation loan can help you pay it off more efficiently. This type of loan combines multiple debts into one loan with a lower interest rate.

3. **Avoid closing old credit accounts:** Closing old credit accounts can shorten the length of your credit history, which can negatively impact your credit score.

4. **Be aware of the impact of credit inquiries:** Hard inquiries, which occur when you apply for new credit, can temporarily lower your credit score. Avoid applying for new credit unless it is absolutely necessary.

5. **Regularly monitor your credit report:** Regularly checking your credit report can help you identify and address any errors or fraudulent activity.

6. **Seek professional help:** If you are struggling to improve your credit score, consider seeking help from a credit counseling agency or a financial advisor.

It's also important to keep in mind that there is no magic solution to fixing bad credit. It takes time, effort, and commitment to improve your credit score. But by understanding the factors that affect your credit score and taking the necessary steps to improve it, you can achieve a good credit score and open up many financial opportunities for you in the future.

In conclusion, bad credit can make it difficult to secure loans or credit cards with favorable terms, but it's not a permanent condition. By understanding the factors that affect your credit score and taking the necessary steps to improve it, you can fix your bad credit and achieve a good credit score. Remember that rebuilding credit takes time and you need to be patient and consistent in your efforts.

Maintaining Good Credit

Once you've built good credit, it's important to maintain it. To keep your credit score high, make sure you continue to make all of your payments on time, keep your credit utilization low, and monitor your credit reports for errors. Maintaining good credit is an ongoing process that requires attention and commitment. Here are a few tips to help you maintain a good credit score:

1. **Pay all of your bills on time:** Late payments can have a major negative impact on your credit score. Make sure you pay all of your bills on time, and set reminders if necessary.

2. **Keep your credit card balances low:** High credit card balances can negatively impact your credit score. Try to keep your credit card balances below 30 percent of your credit limit.

3. **Don't open too many new credit accounts at once:** Opening too many new credit accounts in a short period of time can lower your credit score. Only open new accounts when necessary.

4. **Don't close old credit accounts:** Closing old credit accounts can shorten the length of your credit history, which can negatively impact your credit score.

5. **Monitor your credit report:** Checking your credit report regularly can help you identify and address any errors or fraudulent activity.

6. **Avoid applying for credit you don't need:** Every time you apply for credit, it results in a hard inquiry on your credit report, which can lower your score.

7. **Seek professional help, if necessary:** If you are struggling to maintain a good credit score, consider seeking help from a credit counseling agency or a financial advisor.

Remember that maintaining good credit is a long-term commitment. It takes time and effort to build a good credit score, and it also takes time and effort to maintain it. Stay committed to your financial goals and be mindful of the actions you take in relation to your credit. By following these tips, you can maintain a good credit score and enjoy the many benefits that come with it.

Building and maintaining good credit takes time and effort, but the rewards are well worth it. By following the steps outlined in this ebook, you can take control of your credit and enjoy the many benefits that come with good credit. Remember that the most important thing is to make all of your payments on time, to keep your credit utilization low, and to monitor your credit reports regularly.

ABOUT THE AUTHOR

Josette Hill-Wilson is the Financial Treasurer of the Southeastern Connecticut Chapter of SCORE, a nationwide, nonprofit organization and a resource partner of the U.S. Small Business Administration that offers free advice and mentorship to small-business owners. Josette started her own small business in 2015 when she founded J.A.H Financial Service & Real Estate, a CPA firm she started to help small businesses establish financial accounting and control systems to manage complex financials. Her company is now a household name in Hartford, Connecticut, where she is empowering minority business owners through financial education and access to capital to grow their businesses. Josette Hill is an accomplished CPA and financial advisor. She has received the Life Foundation Award from New York Life and was named the number one Regional Leader at Primerica Financial

Services. Josette Hill has been included in Marquis Who's Who in America magazine, where she was praised for her entrepreneurship. She was also featured in SCORE National Volunteer Spotlight as a financial mentor and leader in her community. Outside of running a successful financial service company, Josette also volunteers her financial education to serve on boards of other organizations such as Taste of the Caribbean Arts and Culture Organization and West Indian Social Club of Hartford, Connecticut. She resides in Portland, Connecticut with her husband, Dean Wilson, and their children.

Printed in the USA
CPSIA information can be obtained
at www.ICGtesting.com
LVHW022150141023
761116LV00005B/106